A LOOK AT THE BILL OF RIGHTS

# Freedom of RELIGION

BY MARY GRIFFIN

CRASHCOURSE

Gareth Stevens PUBLISHING

**Please visit our website, www.garethstevens.com. For a free color catalog of all our high-quality books, call toll free 1-800-542-2595 or fax 1-877-542-2596.**

**Library of Congress Cataloging-in-Publication Data**
Names: Griffin, Mary, 1978- author.
Title: Freedom of religion / Mary Griffin.
Description: Buffalo, New York : Gareth Stevens Publishing, 2026. | Series: A look at the Bill of Rights | Includes index.
Identifiers: LCCN 2024026569 | ISBN 9781482470260 (library binding) | ISBN 9781482470253 (paperback) | ISBN 9781482470277 (ebook)
Subjects: LCSH: Freedom of religion–United States–Juvenile literature. | United States. Constitution. 1st Amendment–Juvenile literature.
Classification: LCC KF4783 .G75 2026 | DDC 342.7308/52–dc23/eng/20240614
LC record available at https://lccn.loc.gov/2024026569

First Edition

Published in 2026 by
**Gareth Stevens Publishing**
2544 Clinton Street
Buffalo, NY 14224



Designer: Andrea Davison-Bartolotta
Editor: Kristen Rajczak Nelson

Photo credits: Cover, p. 1 Mila Supinskaya Glashchenko/Shutterstock.com; series art (interior background texture) Nik Merkulov/Shutterstock.com; series art (fact box sticker) Sulovsky/Shutterstock.com; series art (blue backgrounds) Le Chernina/Shutterstock.com; series art (banners) saicle/Shutterstock.com; p. 5 Dennis MacDonald/Shutterstock.com; p. 7 (Madison) courtesy of Library of Congress; p. 7 (Mason) Everett Collection/Shutterstock.com; p. 9 (bottom) Adam Calaitzis/Shutterstock.com; p. 9 (top) courtesy of National Archives; p. 11 (top left) Nastyaofly/Shutterstock.com; p. 11 (top right) PradeepGaurs/Shutterstock.com; p. 11 (bottom left) Drazen Zigic/Shutterstock.com; p. 11 (bottom right) FS Stock/Shutterstock.com; p. 13 (top) Ted Eytan/Flickr.com; p. 13 (bottom) Trump White House Archived/Flickr.com; p. 14 Prachaya Roekdeethaweesab/Shutterstock.com; p. 15 Sheila Fitzgerald/Shutterstock.com; p. 17 dotshock/Shutterstock.com; p. 19 Torontonian/Alamy Stock Photo; p. 21 Dave Newman/Shutterstock.com; p. 23 Krakenimages.com/Shutterstock.com; p. 25 Studio Romantic/Shutterstock.com; p. 27 SDI Productions/iStockphoto.com; p. 29 Mark Hayes/Shutterstock.com; p. 30 ijaydesign99/Shutterstock.com.



Printed in China

Some of the images in this book illustrate individuals who are models. The depictions do not imply actual situations or events.

CPSIA compliance information: Batch #QS26GS: For further information contact Gareth Stevens at 1-800-542-2595.

# Contents



Words in the glossary appear in **bold** type the first time they are used in the text.

# THE HIGHEST LAW

A constitution lists the most basic laws of a country. The U.S. Constitution is the highest law in the United States. That means all other laws must agree with the Constitution. The first 10 **amendments** to the Constitution are called the Bill of Rights.

**Make the GRADE**

The U.S. Constitution has been in use by the United States since 1789!

# RIGHTS WORRIES

When the Constitution was written, some people didn't think it **protected** the rights of U.S. **citizens** enough. In fact, some leaders didn't want to sign the Constitution without a list of rights added to it! James Madison originally wrote 17 amendments that would address this worry.

James Madison

Make the GRADE

James Madison was a member of Congress from Virginia who later became U.S. president. He based the Bill of Rights in part on the Virginia Declaration of Rights written by George Mason.

George Mason

The states **approved** 10 of the amendments in 1791. Now called the Bill of Rights, these amendments guarantee, or promise, certain freedoms. One of these is the freedom of religion. This right is found in the First Amendment.

Congress of the United States,
begun and held at the City of New-York, on
Wednesday the fourth of March, one thousand seven hundred and eighty nine.

Bill of Rights

**Make the GRADE**

The First Amendment also guarantees the freedom of the press, freedom of speech, and the right to assemble, or gather, peacefully.

# WHAT IS RELIGION?

Religion is the beliefs, rules, and **ceremonies** a group has when honoring a god or gods. In the First Amendment, it says: "Congress shall make no law respecting an establishment of religion, or **prohibiting** the free exercise thereof." What does that mean?

**Make the GRADE**

The first 13 United States started out as English colonies, or land controlled by England. England had a state, or government-backed, religion: the Church of England.

# THE ESTABLISHMENT CLAUSE

The part of the First Amendment that says "Congress shall make no law respecting an establishment of religion" is the Establishment **Clause**. To the Constitution's writers, this meant the U.S. government could not choose one state religion. It also stops the government from showing favor to one religion over another.

Make the GRADE

The Establishment Clause also stops the government from pushing the idea of religion in general—no matter what the faith.

The Establishment Clause is sometimes said to guard the "**separation** of church and state." The most well-known use of this idea comes from a letter President Thomas Jefferson wrote in 1802. He wrote that the Establishment Clause built a "wall of separation between the church and state."

Make the GRADE

The Constitution does not say citizens are promised "separation of church and state." This is a long-used **interpretation** of the Establishment Clause.

# THE FREEDOM TO BELIEVE ...

The First Amendment gives citizens the freedom to be part of any religion they want. They have the right to take part in the practices of that religion. This can be going to church services, praying at certain times, or wearing clothing that has religious meaning.

Make the GRADE

A person's right to speak out about their religion is protected by two parts of the First Amendment, the freedom of religion and the freedom of speech.

# ... OR NOT BELIEVE

The First Amendment protects citizens' rights not to practice any religion too. It guarantees that no person must take part in religious activities. One sentence of the First Amendment has come to mean so much! Its meaning has been further interpreted over the years.

**Make the GRADE**

The Bill of Rights guaranteed citizens' rights under the national government. The Fourteenth Amendment made it so these rights were guaranteed under state governments too.

# THE SUPREME COURT'S JOB

The U.S. Supreme Court is the highest court in the country. One of its jobs is to judge whether laws or actions of presidents, states, and citizens follow the Constitution. Many times, this has meant deciding court cases having to do with the freedom of religion.

**Make the GRADE**

The Supreme Court's ability to judge whether something is unconstitutional—or not following the Constitution—is called judicial review.

Supreme Court Building

# PRAYER IN PUBLIC SCHOOLS

The 1962 Supreme Court case *Engel v. Vitale* looked at whether it was constitutional for public schools to start the day with a prayer. The Supreme Court said this **violated** the Establishment Clause of the First Amendment, even if students could choose not to say the prayer.

Make the GRADE

The judges on the Supreme Court are called justices.

# RELIGIOUS CLUBS AT SCHOOL

In 1990, the Supreme Court upheld a group of students' right to form a **Christian** club in *Westside Community Schools v. Mergens*. The court decided the club didn't violate the Establishment Clause, in part because the club would meet outside of class time.

**Make the GRADE**

The decision in *Westside Community Schools v. Mergens* also upheld a law meant in part to protect student religious groups of any faith.

# PRAYER ON THE FIELD

The Supreme Court still hears cases about freedom of religion! In 2022, *Kennedy v. Bremerton School District* asked if a football coach could pray on the field with students who wanted to. In this case, the court said the coach had the constitutional right to do so.

**Make the GRADE**

A Supreme Court decision may not be unanimous, or something all the justices agree with.

# THE BILL OF RIGHTS TODAY

Freedom of religion is just one of many freedoms guaranteed by the Bill of Rights! This part of the Constitution was written over 230 years ago. How the president, states, and most importantly, the Supreme Court, interpret these have changed so much—and will keep changing.

**Make the GRADE**

The U.S. Constitution begins with the words "We the People." This shows that the power of the Constitution comes from the people of the United States!

# WHAT IS FREEDOM OF RELIGION?

Citizens can believe in any religion they want.

Citizens can take part in religious practices.

Citizens do not have to take part in any religion.

The government cannot establish a state religion.

The government cannot show favor to one religion over another.

# Glossary

**amendment:** A change or addition to a constitution.

**approve:** To give official agreement.

**ceremony:** An event to honor or celebrate something.

**Christian:** Having to do with those who follow the teachings of Jesus Christ.

**clause:** A part of a legal document.

**citizen:** Someone who lives in a country legally and has certain rights.

**interpretation:** An explanation of the meaning of something.

**prohibit:** To stop something from being done.

**protect:** To keep safe.

**separation:** The act of keeping two things separate, or apart, from one another.

**violate:** To do something not allowed by law.

# For More Information

## Books

Matulli, Allison, and Clelia Castro-Malaspina. *Your Freedom, Your Power: A Kid's Guide to the First Amendment.* Philadelphia, PA: Running Press Kids, 2023.

Keppeler, Jill. *What Is the First Amendment?* Buffalo, NY: Rosen Publishing, 2023.

## Website

**First Amendment—Freedom of Religion**
*https://www.annenbergclassroom.org/resource/freedom-of-religion/*
Read about more Supreme Court cases that have shaped what freedom of religion looks like in the United States today.

**Publisher's note to educators and parents:** Our editors have carefully reviewed these websites to ensure that they are suitable for students. Many websites change frequently, however, and we cannot guarantee that a site's future contents will continue to meet our high standards of quality and educational value. Be advised that students should be closely supervised whenever they access the internet.

# Index